Spirit to Spirit

A Twenty-One-Day
Spirit-Awakening Devotional

Arise:

Awake From Your Slumber

TENICKA WASHINGTON

Spirit to Spirit: A Twenty-One Day Spirit-Awakening Devotional

©Copyright 2025 Tenicka Washinton

ISBN: 979-8-9929883-1-4

Scripture quotations marked (NIV) are taken from the Holy Bible, New International Version®, NIV®. Copyright © 1973, 1978, 1984, 2011 by Biblica, Inc.™ Used by permission of Zondervan. All rights reserved worldwide. www.zondervan.comThe "NIV" and "New International Version" are trademarks registered in the United States Patent and Trademark Office by Biblica, Inc.™

Scripture marked NKJV taken from the New King James Version®. Copyright © 1982 by Thomas Nelson. Used by permission. All rights reserved.

Scripture quotations taken from the Amplified® Bible (AMP), Copyright © 2015 by The Lockman Foundation. Used by permission. lockman.org

"Scripture quotations taken from the Amplified® Bible (AMPC), Copyright © 1954, 1958, 1962, 1964, 1965, 1987 by The Lockman Foundation Used by permission. lockman.org"

This devotional is dedicated to my husband,
who has been my joy and strength,
and to our three beautiful children,
who bring us joy each day.

If we live in the spirit, let us also walk in the spirit.

—Galatians 5:25, KJV

*For to be carnally minded is death,
but to be spiritually minded is life and peace.*

—Romans 8:6, KJV

Introduction

This twenty-one-day devotional will help you develop the spiritual aptitude to walk in the Spirit. This devotional is meant to edify, strengthen, and build you up in your spirit. My prayer for everyone who reads this devotional is that the Word of God will move them so that they will come alive in their spirit. That the Word will take deep root and multiply a hundred-fold in their hearts and lives. So many of us Christians are walking around in a spiritual sleep, and I believe that if you stick with this twenty-one-day devotional, God is going to call you out of slumber into a more intimate Spirit-led relationship with Him.

This devotional will prayerfully help you develop an intimate walk with God that is Spirit-led and Spirit-filled. That provokes you to not just be a hearer, but a doer of the Word. At this very moment, God is whispering to you—Spirit to spirit. So, open your heart to hear what God is speaking to you in this season. When you hear God's voice, harden not your heart and allow the Holy Spirit to minister to you, Spirit to spirit.

Day One:
Hands Lifted

May my prayers be set before you like incense; may the lifting up of my hands be like the evening sacrifice.

—Psalm 141:2, NIV

As you go throughout your day, think about how often you have a moment to raise your hands and say, "Thank you, God!" Thank you, God, for your faithfulness. God's Word declares that your worship and praise are a sweet-smelling scent unto God's nose. So, if you haven't taken the time today to say, "thank you, God," take this time to stand in awe of the reigning Savior's sovereignty and say, "thank You" with a pure and devoted heart. Starting your day with praise on your lips will change the outlook of your day. You will become more grateful and filled with thanksgiving as you see God in His awesomeness and make this a daily routine. Your actions toward God won't be a "take, take, and I want" attitude. Instead, it will become an attitude of "If you don't do anything else for me, God, I thank You for just being who You are." You will transition your thinking from earthly pleasures and wants to seeing yourself seated in heavenly places and dwelling on the things that are above and not on the things of this earth. You will set your heart and mind upon heaven with a grateful heart.

Take time to put yourself in a physical stance that says by your actions, "I'm reaching up to You, Father, to tell You that You have been a good, good Father to me. Therefore, I give You all praise and honor with hands lifted to heaven. My posture of worship through the lifting up of my hands shows my heart's devotion and love for our Heavenly Father."

Day Two:
Bear Ye, One Another's Burdens

*Bear ye one another's burdens
and so fulfill the law of Christ.*

—Galatians 6:2, KJV

In these perilous times, I tried to rationalize why someone would commit such atrocities, and I couldn't rationalize it. So, then I began to think, *God, why? Your servant is lamenting. My heart is breaking for those individuals impacted by these perilous times and mass shootings.* Then, God, You brought to my attention Lamentations: "Arise, cry out in the night, as the watches begin; pour out your heart like water in the presence of the Lord. Lift your hands to him for the lives of your children" (Lamentations 2:19, NIV).

I must trust the Lord with my children. I must trust Him with things that I can't control. I must trust Him with the very thing that He gave me. So, I lift my hands in praise and worship, knowing that You have all things in the palm of Your hand. As I began to pray and cry out to God, I know Him to be a mender of the broken-hearted. There are many people hurting, filled with rage, but God says in His Word that "the Lord is nigh unto them that are of a broken heart; and saveth such of a contrite spirit" (Psalm 34:18, KJV). God does not despise a broken and contrite heart.

I may not understand all things, but I do know that You are the sovereign God and a very present help in times of need. You tell us to bear one another's burdens and so fulfill the law of Christ. So, I bear the burdens of all those struggling with pain, hurt, anger, premature death, and uncertainty. God's Word declares that Jesus is our comforter and that He will comfort us in all our afflictions. And that with each tear I cry, You keep a record because You care and love us so much. God's Word declares: "[Cast] all your care upon him, for he cares for you" (1 Peter 5:7, KJV). God tells us to cast our cares upon Him, for He cares for us. So today, I pray to you, God, with outstretched arms, trusting completely in You. I surrender my life to you. I know that I can't make it without you, and my soul thirsts for You in a thirsty land. "I reach out my hands to You; My throat thirsts for You, as a parched land [thirsts for water]" (Psalm 143:6, AMP).

What does parch mean? It means dry land. Things may feel dried around me, but Your presence and anointing will cause living springs and waters to rise in me and those dry places. So, I make a conscious decision to devote my heart to You and raise my hands to You as an expression of worship.

Take this time and lift your hands as an expression of worship to God even with tears flowing down your face, with a heavy heart and uncertainty surrounding us. Know this day that God is greater than any hurt or pain and that He is waiting with outstretched arms to meet you in your dry places. God not only sees our tears, but they move Him.

Day Three:
But Even If...

15 Now when you hear the sound of the horn, flute, zither, lyre, harp, pipe and all kinds of music, if you are ready to fall down and worship the image I made, very good. But if you do not worship it, you will be thrown immediately into a blazing furnace. Then what god will be able to rescue you from my hand?

16 Shadrach, Meshach and Abednego replied to him, "King Nebuchadnezzar, we do not need to defend ourselves before you in this matter. 17 If we are thrown into the blazing furnace, the God we serve is able to deliver us from it, and he will deliver us from Your Majesty's hand. 18 But even if he does not, we want you to know, Your Majesty, that we will not serve your gods or worship the image of gold you have set up."

—Daniel 3:15-18, NIV

I went through a season of hardship in my life. It was one thing after the next, and I didn't understand or couldn't explain why it was happening to me. All I knew in that season was that, during this period, I chose to put my trust in God, and I knew somehow that God was going to work all things for my good. I continued to seek God's face and knew that whatever happened, I was going to trust/rely on God. Even if He didn't do what I was requesting of Him or take me out of the situation. During this season, I had to develop a mentality of "But even if God does not heal me or bring me out, He is still God on the throne, and I trust His judgment and sovereignty in my life." Just like the three Hebrew boys in Daniel 3:16 in the Bible. We see here in this passage in the Bible that Israel is under Babylonian rule. God turned Israel over to Babylonian rule because of Israel breaking the covenant with God and worshipping idols. King Nebuchadnezzar of Babylon created a golden statue and mandated that everyone bow down and worship the golden image he had created. His officials brought to his attention that three of his administrators in his court were refusing to bow to the golden statue, and the king summoned the three Hebrew boys to his court. The three Hebrew boys revealed to the king the reason why they would not bow to the golden statue or compromise. Their faith embodied the "But even if God" mentality that fueled their decision not to bow to this statue. Shadrach, Meshach, and Abednego were grounded in a firm, solid belief that God was more than able to deliver them from the hand of the king and the fiery furnace, but even if God did not deliver them, they still wouldn't compromise the Word of God. They had a "But even if God" mentality that God was going to come through for them. But even if He did not, He was still God on the throne, and that would not change their view of or stance on what God was capable of doing in their lives—but let's personalize that word and say "your life."

I believe that God has given me a Word about completely trusting God in today's world. God has released a Word in this season for you to trust God completely, no matter what your circumstances may look like. God wants you to be confident in His divine authority and power. It is God's nature and character to always honor His Word. We must believe God's Word with confidence and stand on the Word of God. When we find ourselves in a state of hardship, no matter what is going on in our lives, no matter how many circumstances we are facing, we must develop a mindset like the three Hebrew boys that is steadfast, unmovable, and unshakable. That, even if God decided, if He allowed me to go into the fire, He's still good. If God decides to deliver me from the fiery furnace or the situation that I am in, He's still good. I trust God, and I say just like the three Hebrew boys, "But even if God does not deliver me, He is still good. He is still God on the throne." Because trust is a position that we take because of God's faithfulness and consistency, I keep on the path I am on until the Lord tells me otherwise.

Let's look at what the "But even if" faith mentality actually is:

1. They didn't feel a need to defend themselves. God is our defense; we stand on the Word of God. Stay loyal and a person of integrity, and God will fight our battles. He will be our very defense, our shield and buckler, the glory and lifter of our heads.

I don't need to fear man; I fear God. I need to stay true to God's calling, follow His commands for my life, and trust Him with my life.

They believed in the Word of God; they had a relationship with God.

2. Next, it is evident in this scripture that they weren't looking for a way of escape. They trusted God's decision in that crisis, and my question to you today is: Are you trusting God in your moment of crisis, or are you panicking, thinking of a way to get out of your situation? As stated, they were not going to go against God or compromise the Word of God. That would cost them too much. Going against the Word of God was worse than worshipping a golden image and losing their lives. That's why the Bible tells us not to store up our treasures in the earthly realm, where moths and vermin corrupt, where thieves break in and steal (Matthew 6:19,KJV).

3. Trust God. When we trust God, we bring honor to God by following His Word, even if it means we lose everything. But in essence you gain everything in Him in your obedience to God. The Word tells us to hide the Word of God in our hearts so that we don't sin against Him. To trust God, you need to have a firm foundation in the Word of God. The Word of God needs to be deeply rooted in your heart.

Day Four:
Don't DOUBT God!

Jesus replied, "Truly I tell you, if you have faith and do not doubt, not only can you do what was done to the fig tree, but also you can say to this mountain, 'Go, throw yourself into the sea,' and it will be done. 22 If you believe, you will receive whatever you ask for in prayer."

—Matthew 21:21-22, NIV

But when you ask, you must believe and not doubt, because the one who doubts is like a wave of the sea, blown and tossed by the wind. ⁷ That person should not expect to receive anything from the Lord. ⁸ Such a person is double-minded and unstable in all they do.

—James 1:6-8, NIV

As I was sitting on my recliner listening to music, God spoke so plainly to me about doubt. How many times in life have you doubted yourself? Some doubts have caused us not to live to our full potential and walk in the full purpose and plan that God has for our lives. Because of doubt, we may have sabotaged relationships, careers, and even our relationship with God. Doubt shows up in our lives through our insecurities and our inability to trust God. When I looked up the definition of doubt, doubt is defined, according to the King James Dictionary, as a lack of belief or confidence in something.

Did you know that doubt can negatively impact your faith because it causes us not to trust and rely on God? In essence, when we doubt God, we are relying on our own strength and reasoning and not on God's supernatural strength and sovereignty.

God can't do anything with your doubt. God moves in our lives when we trust Him and believe that He can do whatever He has promised and spoken over us. Whatever you are believing God for today, trust that He is going to perform it if God speaks His Word. He says that His Word will not return unto Him void, but will accomplish what He has desired for it to accomplish. God's Word is sure and established forever and settled in heaven. If He spoke it, He will do it. So, you should stand firm, unmoved in firm belief that God is going to fulfill His Word. And He says that His Word is flawless, just like silver being purified in a crucible, just like gold refined seven times. God says, "...He watches over His Word to perform it" (paraphrased Jeremiah 1:12, ASV). Then He reassures us and says: "My covenant I will not break, nor alter the thing that is gone out of my lips" (Psalms 89:34, KJV).

If God speaks, it is done. No devil in hell can reverse or hinder the Word of God over your life and prevent you from accomplishing what God has spoken over you. The enemy knows that, so what he does is place doubt into our minds to disarm us and weaken our faith. Because he knows that doubt can hinder or delay the Word of God from coming to complete fruition in our lives. Once doubt creeps in, then it gives the enemy a place to work. Don't let doubt creep in. Meditate on God's Word day and night, believing and being fully persuaded that God is able to do what He has promised. Let God be your confidence. Even when you may not feel confident, you should stand reassured that God will not fail nor forsake you. Stand firm in the Word of God. King David puts it this way: "I have never seen the righteous forsaken nor their seed begging bread" (paraphrased Psalm 37:25).

God is not a God that He should lie. "God is not a man, that He should lie, nor a son of man that he should repent. Has He said, and will He not do? Or has He spoken, and will he not make good?" (Numbers 23:19, KJV). If God said it, it is so. Sometimes, you must keep repeating what God has promised and not give up hope. Choose to trust God and His Word. Remember that God is for you, not against you, and that He is working all things after the counsel of His will and for your good. Don't let your doubt get in the way of what God wants to do in your life. Don't let doubt cause you to be tossed to and fro with every wind of doctrine as a wave in the sea.

Day Five:
Open Your Mouth

> *³¹ And the multitude rebuked them, because they should hold their peace: but they cried the more, saying, Have mercy on us, O Lord, thou son of David.*
>
> *³² And Jesus stood still, and called them, and said, What will ye that I shall do unto you?*
>
> *³³ They say unto him, Lord, that our eyes may be opened.*
>
> *³⁴ So Jesus had compassion on them and touched their eyes: and immediately their eyes received sight, and they followed him.*
>
> —Matthew 20:31-34, KJV

God knows what we have need of before we ask it, but He wants us to open our mouths and speak it. So that we can show we trust and have faith in His position and power. Jesus knew their infirmity but wanted them to be specific with their desire and wants from God. Their actions and faith caused God to have mercy on these two blind men. Sometimes, we must persist and get loud with God to let Him know that we need Him to perform a miracle in our lives. The crowd—the enemy—wants you to be silent, but God is telling you to open your mouth to receive healing, redemption, deliverance, and a Word from God. Open your mouth and tell God what you need so that He can move in your life. Don't miss your blessing or healing because you kept your mouth closed when you should be yelling, "Have mercy on me, oh, Lord!" Once you open your mouth, God will move powerfully in your life.

Day Six:
Don't Neglect Praying for One Another

Therefore confess your sins to each other and pray for each other so that you may be healed. The prayer of a righteous person is powerful and effective.

—James 5:16, NIV

As the end draws near, stay steadfast, unmovable, unwavering, and fervent in prayer. We must stay fervent and disciplined in prayer, as the end-time biblical prophecies fall into place. It is our job as Christians, according to Galatians 6:2 (KJV): "Bear ye one another's burdens and so fulfill the law of Christ." And how we bear one another's burden is through prayer and by actively carrying out the Word of Christ.

When I look over my life, the number one thing that kept me during tribulations, deep pain, receiving healing, deliverance, and staying faith-based was prayer. I realized at an early age that prayer was powerful and that I couldn't do it on my own. I need you, Jesus, and I reach your throne by praying. I completely put my trust in you by praying. This is how I surrender my will to yours. I pray daily that God will incline his ears to my prayers. I am confident that I am praying God's will for my life and others' and not my own will for theirs or my life.

The key to getting prayers answered is being in alignment with God. I am in alignment with God when I am seeking the Lord's face through His Word and worship daily. When I fall out of alignment and connection to God, I pray that I quickly get back into alignment with God by confessing my sins and asking Him to cleanse me of all unrighteousness. As I draw near to God, I begin to resemble him in my speech, words, and actions. I am transformed from the inside out. I pray that His grace will cover me and that I live a righteous life before Him, meaning that I am in right standing with God, not on my own merits, but because of the grace of the Lord. Once I stand assured in this, I know my prayers will be effective and reach the ears of the Lord. Then I can go boldly before the throne of grace to obtain grace and mercy in a time of need with confidence and humility, believing that my prayers will be answered. I strongly believe that as Christians, we should stand on the Word of God and use His Word to pray for one another. How does that look? I ask the Holy Spirit to direct me to scripture that addresses the prayer needs of others and pray that scripture with the Holy Spirit directing and leading me, knowing that God's Word will not come back to Him void, but will accomplish what it is meant to accomplish. So, stay fervent in prayer for one another and watch the Lord miraculously answer your prayers.

Day Seven:
Praying from a Place of Peace

You will guard him and keep him in perfect and constant peace whose mind [both its inclination and its character] is stayed on You, because he commits himself to You, leans on You, and hopes confidently in You.

—Isaiah 26:3, AMPC

God states in His Word that He will guard us and keep us in perfect peace, those whose minds are stayed on Him. Those that trust him. Well, what does that mean? God is saying that if you keep your mind on Him, He will be your sufficiency. He will be your very peace. So, when you face situations, tribulations, and disturbances in your life, don't lose your peace. God is saying that during your storm, you can trust that the battle is already won and He's got your back. So, you don't have to lose your peace; you just have to trust Him and speak His Word, the Word of God, back to Him in your situation. God wants you to be still and know that He is God. He's got everything in the palm of His hand. Keep your mind on Him, and He will give you peace and take care of the situation. He will guide you through whatever storm that is trying to steal your peace. The Word declares that even the winds and waves obey God. So, I know if He can calm the winds and waves in a storm, He can keep me in perfect peace in the midst of whatever storms I am facing. God will always honor His Word. So, today, make this your declaration and decree that you will keep your mind fixed and focused on Him by meditating on the Word day and night, worshipping, praying, and staying in fellowship with Him.

And let the peace of God guard your heart and mind. The Word declares that the mind set on the flesh is death, but the mind set on the spirit is life and peace. I need God to keep my mind in perfect peace so that I can handle situations that are thrown at me during the day. When I am walking in a peaceful state, I trust that God is working his good and perfect will into my life. God has plans to prosper us and not to harm us. The Word declares in Jeremiah 29:11 (NIV): "For I know the plans I have for you, declares the Lord, plans to prosper you and not to harm you, plans to give you hope and a future."

So, on this day, let the peace of God guard your heart and mind as we stay fixed on Him, who He is, and His goodness.

Day Eight:
Do You Know the Father's Voice?

³ The gatekeeper opens the gate for him, and the sheep listen to his voice. He calls his own sheep by name and leads them out.

⁴ When he has brought out all his own, he goes on ahead of them, and his sheep follow him because they know his voice.

⁵ But they will never follow a stranger; in fact, they will run away from him because they do not recognize a stranger's voice.

—John 10:3-5, NIV

Do you know the Father's voice? This is my question to you today. Or is God's voice drowned out by a stranger's voice and your desire to achieve worldly pleasures? God's Word declares that those who follow Him, meaning His children, know His voice and they will not follow a stranger. When I think about this scripture, I think about a time when my children were infants, and I would enter the house after being gone a while, and once they heard my voice, my husband would say he knew I was in the house because my children's eyes would light up and they would smile. If another person whom my children were not familiar with entered the house and began to talk, they would not get the same reaction.

When we know the voice of the Father, we respond by our actions and follow Him in word and deed. Are you sensitive to the voice of God? To be sensitive to the voice of God, we must have an intimate relationship with God. The Word says that if you draw nigh unto God, He will draw nigh unto you. I draw nigh unto God by praying—seeking His face—reading, meditating on the Word of God day and night, memorizing scriptures and applying them to my daily life, and walking in constant communion and praise to God. One way that you will know the voice of the Father is by being a hearer and doer of the Word of God. When we don't know God's voice, we will follow a stranger's voice and the deceits of the enemy. The main goal of the enemy is to deceive and blind the minds of saints. Intimacy with God causes me to know his voice. Knowing and reading the Word of God helps me hear and know what the voice of the Father sounds like.

> *[14] And no marvel; for Satan himself*
> *is transformed into an angel of light.*
>
> —*2 Corinthians 11:14, KJV*

The enemy transforms from an angel of dark to an angel of light. That means that the enemy at times will sound like the father, but don't be misled. You have to check the source and the fruit behind the voice. It also, means that the enemy will take the truth and slightly twist it to deceive us. We must make sure that in these end days, we are following the voice of God and are not being tossed to and fro with every wind of doctrine of a stranger's voice. The Word declares in Ephesians 4:14 (KJV) "that we henceforth be no longer children, tossed to and fro and carried about with every wind of doctrine by the sleight of men and their cunning and craftiness, whereby they lie in wait to deceive."

Make this a declaration today that you will only follow the voice of God and not a stranger's voice.

Day Nine:
Walk with Me

When thou passest through the waters, I will be with thee; and through the rivers, they shall not overflow thee: when thou walkest through the fire, thou shalt not be burned; neither shall the flame kindle upon thee.

—*Isaiah 43:2, KJV*

This is the day that you are going to make a commitment to God and draw nigh unto Him and put aside everything that is drawing you away from the love of the Father and walking with Him. God's Word declares in James 4:8 (KJV): "Draw near to God, and He will draw near to you." Today, God is saying, "Walk with Me." For when you walk with God, He will lead and direct you. He will give you knowledge, wisdom, and understanding in all things. The Word declares in Isaiah 30:21 (KJV): "And thine ears shall hear a word behind thee, saying, this is the way, walk ye in it, when ye turn to the right hand, and when ye turn to the left."

God is saying He will give you direction and insight into things you don't even know about. All we must do is walk with Him. God desires to be known; He wants to be close to us. That's why He tells us to call Him Immanuel, meaning "God with us." For when we walk with God, we find His safety, protection, and shepherding. God wants you to pray and seek His face. God is relational; He wants to form a relationship with us. God is saying that if you walk with Him, He will be all you need. Ask yourself today, are you walking with God? Because He wants to walk with you. When we make a conscious decision to walk with God, He will never leave us or forsake us. He will always be with you, no matter what circumstance you find yourself in.

Day Ten:
How to Change God's Mind

¹ In those days was Hezekiah sick unto death. And the prophet Isaiah the son of Amoz came to him, and said unto him, Thus saith the Lord, Set thine house in order; for thou shalt die, and not live.

² Then he turned his face to the wall, and prayed unto the Lord, saying,

³ I beseech thee, O Lord, remember now how I have walked before thee in truth and with a perfect heart, and have done that which is good in thy sight. And Hezekiah wept sore.

⁴ And it came to pass, afore Isaiah was gone out into the middle court, that the word of the Lord came to him, saying,

⁵ Turn again, and tell Hezekiah the captain of my people, Thus saith the Lord, the God of David thy father, I have heard thy prayer, I have seen thy tears: behold, I will heal thee: on the third day thou shalt go up unto the house of the Lord.

⁶ And I will add unto thy days fifteen years; and I will deliver thee and this city out of the hand of the king of Assyria; and I will defend this city for mine own sake, and for my servant David's sake.

—2 Kings 20:1-6, KJV

Did you know that God can change the course of His plan for your life and destiny because of your fervent, heartfelt prayers? God can be set to complete one course of action and change His mind. Prayer is one thing that touches the heart of God. Prayer moves our Heavenly Father to the point that He inclines His ears to our prayers. He will show Himself strongly in our lives and what we are going through for those whose hearts are loyal to Him. And I think to myself, why is that? As I was reading the scripture, God revealed to me that He is relational, and He is touched by what we are touched by. That's how much He loves and cares for us. He gave His only begotten Son so that whosoever believes in Him shall not perish but have everlasting life. We can change God's mind through fervent, heartfelt prayer that is fueled by our intimacy with Christ. When writing this article, I was directed to 2 Kings 20:1-6 (KJV) with the prophet Isaiah and King Hezekiah. The prophet Isaiah was asked to go tell King Hezekiah to get his affairs in order because he was going to succumb to his illness. When the prophet tells King Hezekiah this and leaves the room, King Hezekiah cries out to God and begins to pray, and God tells the prophet Isaiah to go back and tell the king that He has heard his prayer. That he will not succumb to his illness and that God will add fifteen years to his life!

Fervent, heartfelt prayers will move God and touch His heart to the point that He will change His mind or course of action. Heartfelt prayers will cause God to remember you and change His course for your life. Just think that my prayers, your prayers, have the ability to change the mind of the sovereign God. That's how much God loves and cares for us. David puts it this way in Psalm 8:4 (KJV): "What is mankind that you are mindful of them, human beings that you care for them."

So today, place yourself at the mercy of God and watch Him intervene on your behalf. Another important point that the Holy Spirit highlighted to me in this passage was that Hezekiah prayed that God would remember him. To remember how he walked wholeheartedly and faithfully before God. Sometimes, we need to pray, "God, Remember Me! Because when You remember me, surely You will have mercy upon me and bless me. That You will turn the impossible into the possible. Oh, Lord, remember Your servant today."

Day Eleven:
Keep Knocking, Keep Praying

^{12} When this had dawned on him, he went to the house of Mary the mother of John, also called Mark, where many people had gathered and were praying. ^{13} Peter knocked at the outer entrance, and a servant named Rhoda came to answer the door. ^{14} When she recognized Peter's voice, she was so overjoyed she ran back without opening it and exclaimed, "Peter is at the door!"

^{15} "You're out of your mind," they told her. When she kept insisting that it was so, they said, "It must be his angel."

^{16} But Peter kept on knocking, and when they opened the door and saw him, they were astonished.

—Acts 12:12-16, NIV

Sometimes, we get to a place in our prayer life where we stop pushing and fervently praying for a situation because we feel there is no hope or we are just tired of the situation we are in. And I question if Peter was at that point when he was placed in prison by King Herod. Naturally, Peter didn't see a way out of his situation. The Word didn't say that Peter was praying when he was placed in prison, but the scriptures did say that the church was earnestly praying to God for Peter.

Peter was miraculously released from prison on the prayers of believers. Peter was sleeping, and the angel woke him up to lead him out of prison. So, this tells me that prayer on behalf of another is powerful. Somebody's release, blessing, and miracle are in your prayer. No matter what the situation may look like, just keep praying. Peter was surrounded by soldiers and lying in between two soldiers when God miraculously sent an angel to rescue him from his situation. His situation looked bleak, but God would make the impossible possible.

Sometimes, we pray for things and don't believe that God has answered and heard our prayers. And I think of this story with the apostle Peter, who was miraculously released from prison by an angel.

So, my message to you today is to keep knocking, meaning keep praying until God answers your prayer. Pray with fervency and urgency. God's Word declares in Isaiah 46:4 (NIV): "Even to your old age and gray hairs, I am he, I am he who will sustain you. I have made you and I will carry you; I will sustain you and I will rescue you."

God declares in His Word that He will sustain and rescue us when we find ourselves in trouble. God is the bridge over troubled waters—just like he did with Peter in the prison. King Herod had Peter sent to prison and guarded by four squads of four soldiers each, and Peter fell asleep between two soldiers. When Peter realized that he had been released from prison by an angel, he went to the place where they were praying and began to knock on the door. Rhoda, being overjoyed, didn't open the door and went back to tell everybody that Peter was at the door. The Bible says in Acts 12:14-16 (NIV) that they, the people praying for Peter, did not believe her.

How many times has God answered our prayers or sent people to us, and out of our disbelief or lack of faith, we couldn't receive it? We must know beyond a shadow of a doubt that God answers prayers. So, I charge you today to keep praying, interceding on behalf of a loved one or yourself, and watch God miraculously come through for you.

Day Twelve:
Overcoming Fear

For God has not given us a spirit of fear but of power, and of love and a sound mind.

—2 Timothy 1:7, NKJV

It seems like nowadays, fear is taking hold of so many people to the point that it is debilitating and creates hopelessness. But God came to give us hope and to give us a peace that surpasses our understanding.

Today, we must declare and decree that we have power over those things that cause us to fear. The Word says in Luke 10:19 (KJV): "Behold, I give unto you power to tread upon serpents and scorpions, and over all the powers of the enemy: and nothing by any means shall hurt you." God has given us power over our fears and the ones that cause us to fear. Fear is not bigger than our God, and we must hold and speak this word over our situations and fears. So, whatever spirit of fear is tormenting you, pray that God will replace it with hope and love.

The Bible says that God has given us a spirit of love, meaning that when we are afraid, we need to conquer fear with love. The King James Bible says in 1 John 4:18: "There is no fear in love; but perfect love casteth out fear: because fear hath torment. He that feareth is not made perfect in love."

Perfect love casts out fear. So, if fear is taking hold in my life, there are some areas where love is not fully present, because love casts out fear. God is talking about true agape, unconditional love, which casts out fear. We know as Christians that God has a good and perfect plan for each one of us. A plan not to harm us but to prosper us. God is for us, not against us. So, why fear when we know that God has us in the palm of His hands?

Last, the Word says that God has given us a sound mind. I have a sound mind, which means that the peace of God trumps all the situations in my life that causes me to fear. The Bible says in John 14:27 (NIV): "Peace I leave you; my peace I give you. Peace I do not give to you as the world gives. Do not let your hearts be troubled and do not be afraid."

Let this message cast out every spirit of fear that is holding you back.

Day Thirteen:
Isolated Fear

¹ Ahab told Jezebel everything Elijah had done. He told her how Elijah had killed all the prophets of Baal with his sword. ² So Jezebel sent a message to Elijah. She said, "You can be sure that I will kill you, just as I killed the other prophets. I'll do it by this time tomorrow. If I don't, may the gods punish me greatly."

³ Elijah was afraid. So he ran for his life. When he came to Beersheba in Judah, he left his servant there, ⁴ while he himself went a day's journey into the wilderness. He came to a broom bush, sat down under it and prayed that he might die. "I have had enough, Lord," he said. "Take my life; I am no better than my ancestors." ⁵ Then he lay down under the bush and fell asleep.

⁹ There he went into a cave and spent the night.

—1 Kings 19:1-5, 9, NIV

We see here in this passage of scripture that once Ahab told Jezebel all the things the prophet Elijah had done, it infuriated her to the point that she sent a messenger to threaten the life of the prophet.

And that's just like the strategy of the enemy: once he hears about the glory of God in your life, sees that you are chosen and called to walk in the power of the Lord, he will send a messenger to threaten you. The Word declares in 1 Peter 5:8 (NIV): "Be alert and of sober mind. Your enemy, the devil, prowls around like a roaring lion looking for someone to devour." The emphasis in this scripture is that the enemy prowls around like a roaring lion. It doesn't say that he is a roaring lion but that he acts like one. The enemy uses fear to try to hinder you from walking in the call of God in your life. To prevent you from doing what God called you to do, the enemy will instill fear in you to threaten you. In this context, how can we connect this story to our lives? Well think of Jezebel, metaphorically representing anything in your life that is threatening you, manipulating and trying to instill fear in your life. Jezebel is that external voice that causes internal fear within you. Today, think about what those external threats are that the enemy is speaking into your ear and that are causing fear within you. Those external threats that are paralyzing you from walking in the call of God in your life. Today, is the day to address those empty threats with the Word of God. For the Word declares in 2 Timothy 1:7 (KJV): "For God hath not given us the spirit of fear; but of power, and of love, and of a sound mind." We see here that the prophet was consumed with fear, and when we live in the Spirit, God does not want us to be consumed with fear, but wants us to walk and trust His sovereignty and power.

We see here that Jezebel's words are just an empty threat to the prophet, because she sends a messenger to the prophet who says that by this time tomorrow, she will kill him. But if she was authorized to take his life, she would not have sent a messenger to him; she would have sent the king's guards to take his life at that very moment. But Elijah was not able to see this revelation and ran away in fear of the words that were spoken to him. He was so afraid that he took shelter in a cave.

When you find yourself in a cave with Jezebel's words tormenting you—Jezebel's voice represents anything in your life that is tormenting, intimidating, and causing fear within you—remember:

1) God's faithfulness and consistency; think of those Mount Carmel moments.

Think about the demonstration of God's power in your life. Think about the times when He made a way out of no way, healed your body, and walked with you through the valley of the shadow of death. The times when God prepared a table before you in the presence of your enemies. How He scattered your enemies in front of you. And how He has anointed and chosen you before the foundation of the world.

2) Remember God is always with you. God says He will never leave you nor forsake you. Don't forsake God because He will not forsake you.

3) Get out of your head. One of the strategies of the enemy is to instill fear in your mind. Because what he wants to do, God has not authorized him to do in your life, so he puts fear into your mind to make you self-sabotage or destroy your life. Remember that the enemy must get authorization from God before he can act in our lives. Look at the story of Job, when God says to Satan, "Have you considered my servant, Job?"

4) God says, "I will be with you always, so if you make your bed in hell, I'm with you." If you make your bed in a cave, God will be the whisper that draws you out of the cave.

5) Every word the enemy speaks to assassinate my purpose and instill fear in me, God will cast down with a still calm voice. I can stand with confidence in the very fact that God will never leave or forsake me. When I am walking in the Spirit, God will give me direction. For the Word declares in Isaiah 30:21 (KJV): "And thine ears shall hear a word behind thee, saying, This is the way, walk ye in it, when ye turn to the right hand, and when ye turn to the left." God will speak a word to me that comforts and gives me hope. A word to elevate me out of my state of fear.

In times of fear, God will not only guide you, but He will protect you while you are hurting and isolating yourself in the cave. I know you're hurt and distraught but get up and eat (meaning get in his presence, by reading the word and praying). Get in His presence, and you will find rest and strength.

Day Fourteen:
Hold Your Peace

¹⁹ And the angel answering said unto him, "I am Gabriel, that Stand in the presence of God; and am sent to speak unto thee, and to shew thee these glad tidings. ²⁰ And, behold, thou shalt be dumb, and not able to speak, until the day that these things shall be performed, because thou believest not my words, which shall be fulfilled in their season."

—Luke 1:19-20, KJV

Some things that the Lord speaks to us are so powerful that He does not want our doubts, disbelief, and words to sabotage the very purpose and mission that He is going to accomplish in our lives. So, God will silence you until that work is fulfilled in your life. For most of us, that will be a spiritual silence or delay. Meaning that you don't see an immediate manifestation of God's Word, but God will delay the Word until we are spiritually ready and mature for the Word to come to fruition in our lives. We will see the full completion of God's Word when we fully believe, are spiritually ready, and our words align with what God is promising us. Our words must align with the very thing that God is speaking over our lives, and disbelief will hinder the very work God is trying to accomplish in our lives. That is why the angel silenced Zechariah. For Zechariah, that was a physical silence. We see this here in the text with Zechariah and the angel Gabriel. God sent the angel to give Zechariah a Word from God that his wife, Elizabeth, of old age, will have a baby boy, and he will be great in the sight of God, and that he is to name the baby John. Zechariah did not believe the angel's words, and due to his unbelief, he was silenced. Look at Luke 1:20 (KJV): Zechariah's mouth was shut by the angel of God and was not open until he was obedient to God. And named the child John. It was custom to name the firstborn after the father or another relative. However, God selected the child's name and wanted to make sure that the name spoken by the angel would be given to the child. Once Zechariah names the child, his mouth is opened (Luke 1:59-65, NIV). This story illustrates that there are some circumstances in our lives in which obedience is so important to God that He will shut our mouths so that our words do not hinder what God desires to do in our lives and the lives of those connected to you. God requires obedience and belief in the words He speaks to us.

When we receive a Word from God, we need to hear, receive, believe, and obey the words that God is speaking over our lives. Then we need to speak and make an outward confession of that Word in our lives. God says that in our tongues, there is the power of life and death. And God tells us to choose life. We want to make sure that when we receive a Word from God, we will speak what God speaks and believe His Word. That is why words, your belief system, are so important to God. God has to trust you with His Word. God honors and keeps every Word He speaks because that is His nature. He is a covenant-keeping God. When God questions our ability to believe His Word, that is when He will silence us because the great work He is working in our lives is so important that He does not want us to sabotage or cast doubt on the very completion of that work. No Word from God will ever fail, but we can hinder the work of God in our lives through our words and unbelief.

Day Fifteen:
Rooted in God

So then, just as you received Christ Jesus as Lord, continue to live your lives in him,⁷ rooted and built up in him, strengthened in the faith as you were taught, and overflowing with thankfulness.

—*Colossians 2:6-7, NIV*

"Therefore everyone who hears these words of mine and puts them into practice is like a wise man who built his house on the rock. ²⁵ The rain came down, the streams rose, and the winds blew and beat against that house; yet it did not fall, because it had its foundation on the rock. ²⁶ But everyone who hears these words of mine and does not put them into practice is like a foolish man who built his house on sand. ²⁷ The rain came down, the streams rose, and the winds blew and beat against that house, and it fell with a great crash."

— *Matthew 7:24-27, NIV*

When we are rooted in God, we are not tossed to and fro with every wind of doctrine. Jesus becomes our sure foundation; He is our rock, our stable ground, and our firm foundation. So, when we are faced with tribulations, trials, and demonic attacks, we are not moved or swayed because we are deeply rooted in God. Our roots, when we face tribulation, should deepen, meaning go deeper in the ground. When we are faced with trials, our roots should dig deeper into the ground because we are relying on the one we put our trust in. We don't have shallow roots that can easily be plucked up.

How do we become rooted in God?

1) Staying Connected to the Vine, Jesus: Reading and asking for revelation of the Word (John 15:4-5).

2) Walking in love: "That Christ may dwell in your hearts by faith; that ye, being rooted and grounded in love..." (Ephesians 3:17-20, KJV).

3) Renewing our minds daily. Think about what you are thinking about, and if it is contrary to the Word, bring it into submission to the Word of God.

> *Do not conform to the pattern of this world, but be transformed by the renewing of your mind. Then you will be able to test and approve what God's will is—his good, pleasing and perfect will.*
>
> *—Romans 12:2, NIV*

> *[5] Casting down imaginations, and every high thing that exalteth itself against the knowledge of God, and bringing into captivity every thought to the obedience of Christ;*
>
> *—2 Corinthians 10:5, KJV*

4) Living in the Spirit. "So I say, walk by the Spirit, and you will not gratify the desires of the flesh. [17] For the flesh desires what is contrary to the Spirit, and the Spirit what is contrary to the flesh. They are in conflict with each other, so that you are not to do whatever you want. [18] But if you are led by the Spirit, you are not under the law" (Galatians 5:16-18, NIV).

Live a life that is submitted to God and led by the Spirit so that your soul (mind, will, and emotions) are submitted to God and led by the Spirit, leaving no room for the flesh to rule over you.

5) Praying. "Devote yourselves to prayer, being watchful and thankful" (Colossians 4:2, NIV).

Day Sixteen:

Where Are You? The Absence of Those You Love

About three in the afternoon Jesus cried out in a loud voice, "Eli, Eli, lema sabachthani
[My God, my God, why have you forsaken me]?"

—Matthew 27:46, NIV

Jesus is on the cross, redeeming mankind, and now He is at a lowly point. The point where He felt forsaken by His Father and His disciples. For three years, they tarried with Jesus, and when He needed them the most, they were nowhere to be found.

And the presence of His supernatural Father seems to be quiet at a time when He needs to feel Him or hear Him speak. So, He cries out, "Father, Father, why hast thou forsaken me? It's not enough that one of my friends betrayed me with the very intimacy of a kiss, and the only disciple at the crucifixion was John, staring from far off." And we read that Peter is warming himself by a fire and then denies Jesus thrice. Isn't this just like people when we need them the most? At times, you can't find anybody by your side. And you find yourself in the garden of Gethsemane in agony, laying all your vulnerabilities down at the feet of the Father, transitioning to another point of isolation and absence of the ones you love on the cross. Lamenting, crying out for your Father to show that He is there. In these very moments of distress, that's when God is carrying us. That's when we must know that God's purpose is bigger than our distress. When we are being tested and tried, we have to go through this season alone, just like when we are taking an exam. Before the exam, you prepare and get ready for the test, and on the test day, it's just you. And when we are tested and tried, that's when God is calling our faith to the stand. So, we may feel alone, but God is always with us. In some seasons of our lives, we have to experience His silence to experience His elevation and power in our lives.

When we are tried and pass the test, that's when we move to the next level in Christ. Just like in Job 23:10 (KJV): "God knows the way the righteous shall take and when he is tried, he will come forth as gold." In the testing, I may feel alone; that's when God is pruning me and refining me in the fire and getting rid of all the impurities and dead branches in my life that are hindering me from living a fruitful life and being elevated to the next level in my spiritual growth. When I feel alone, I have to believe God's Word in Joshua 1:5 that God will "never fail thee nor forsake thee." That He is always with me. Even at times when I can't hear or feel him, He's there. Some trials in life we have to go through by ourselves. In those moments, God is not absent from us. He is just silent.

Day Seventeen:
Surrounded!

¹⁵ When the servant of the man of God got up and went out early the next morning, an army with horses and chariots had surrounded the city. "Oh no, my lord! What shall we do?" the servant asked.

¹⁶ "Don't be afraid," the prophet answered. "Those who are with us are more than those who are with them."

¹⁷ And Elisha prayed, "Open his eyes, Lord, so that he may see." Then the Lord opened the servant's eyes, and he looked and saw the hills full of horses and chariots of fire all around Elisha.

—*2 Kings 6:15-17, NIV*

We are living in a day and age that feels like we are surrounded by the enemy. The enemy thinks he has you. Today, we have to decree and declare that we will see the salvation of the Lord in the land of the living. No circumstance or situation is greater than God. I don't care what the situation may feel or look like; God has all things in the palm of His hand. I'm seated in heavenly places. And God is going to come through for me.

When I'm surrounded, that's when God is going to show Himself strong in my life. The enemy thinks he has me surrounded, but God and His angels have the enemy surrounded. Just like he did with Moses and the Israelites and here in this passage with the prophet Elisha. You can be in the center of God's will and still be stuck in what may appear to be a seemingly hopeless situation. That's when God is going to flex a muscle and show Himself strong on behalf of those whose hearts are loyal to Him, and we will see the salvation of the Lord. The Bible declares in 2 Chronicles 16:9: "The eyes of the Lord travel to and fro throughout the whole earth to show himself strong on behalf of those whose heart is loyal to him."

Don't get stuck in fear because the enemy has you surrounded. When the enemy comes in like a flood, the Spirit of God will raise a standard against the enemy. There is nothing to fear when you are in the will of God. He is covering, backing, and surrounding you. Greater is he that is within you than he that is in the world. Our God is too great, too big, too powerful to be defeated.

God is doing things in your life that are sending fear into the hearts of your enemies. Every time He heals you, redeems you from destruction, brings you out of a situation that is hopeless, heals your mind from depression, or delivers you from your enemies, God is showing Himself strong in your life!

Day Eighteen:
Awaken to the Call of God on Your Life

⁹ How long will you lie there, you sluggard?
When will you get up from your sleep?

¹⁰ A little sleep, a little slumber,
a little folding of the hands to rest.

—Proverbs 6:9-10, NIV

Therefore, He says, "Awake, you who sleep,
Arise from the dead, And Christ will give you light."

—Ephesians 5:14, NKJV

A lot of Christians are walking through life in a spiritual sleep, and God is calling you out of sleep to pursue the things of Him. A wise man works wisely. A wise man can discern when it's a season to press in and work hard and when to relax. He knows when to store food and when to reap a harvest in the appropriate seasons. And in our walk with God, He desires for us to know when we need to fast more, pray harder, and diligently seek the things of the kingdom. It has been numerous times in my walk with God that in certain seasons of my life, God would place a burden on me to pray for a particular thing and then remove that burden. Or God would wake me up in the early morning hours to pray and read my Bible, then He would release that burden. We enter different seasons in our lives, and we should know when it's time to work diligently, focus, and fix our eyes directly on what God desires or if it is a season in which we are reaping a harvest. God desires for you to awaken to the things of Him.

The Word declares in Hebrews 11:6 (KJV): "But without faith it is impossible to please him: for he that cometh to God must believe that he is. And that he is a rewarder of them that diligently seek him." When you seek something, you are going after it. You are pursuing something, and that requires work. However, a lot of us are not pursuing God, because we are in a spiritual sleep.

These several indicators show you are in a Spiritual Sleep:

1) Inability to pray. A prayerless man is a weak man. When you find it difficult to pray, then your spirit man, is not awakened to the things of God, and you are not alert and walking in the spirit.

2) Inability to read the Bible. Reading the Word connects you to the things of God. When I read the Word, I gain wisdom, knowledge, understanding, and a revelation of God. My faith is built up. I find strength and strategies to walk in the spirit and not in the flesh. This is how I learn how to discern the voice of God and the voice of the enemy.

3) Not having the desire to fast. When I stop fasting, the flesh takes control of my soul, and the spirit is no longer in control of my soul—mind, will, and emotions. This is a dangerous place to be in. The Word declares in Romans 8:6 (KJV): "For to be carnally minded is death; but the mind of the spirit is life and peace." The Word also declares that it is with the mind that we serve the Lord. But if I am submitted to the flesh, then I am not living an abundant life in the spirit.

Living in a state of spiritual sleepiness is dangerous for Christians because when you're in this state, you will have a difficult time discerning the voice of God because you lack intimacy with Him. You are doing nothing to fuel your fire and relationship with the Father. A little sleep and a little slumber will continue to pull you away from the call and intimacy with God. A little sleep and a little slumber will dampen your spirit, man, and you will eventually fall into a spiritual sleep. Your spirit, man, is no longer awakened to the voice of God, and you will begin to listen to a stranger's voice and not realize it.

Awake from your slumber, you who sleep.

Day Nineteen:

Tap In

*I say then: Walk in the Spirit,
and you shall not fulfill the lust of the flesh.*

17 For the flesh lusts against the Spirit, and the Spirit against the flesh; and these are contrary to one another, so that you do not do the things that you wish.

—Galatians 5:16-17, NKJV

Fight the good fight of the faith. Take hold of the eternal life to which you were called when you made your good confession in the presence of many witnesses.

—1 Timothy 6:12, NIV

God is calling us to tap in. When I was a kid, I used to watch wrestling, and in a tag team fight, once a wrestler wanted to indicate they were tired and needed out, they would tap their partner, the one sitting in the corner who was refreshed and ready to fight and give the other a break to recoup. Some of our brethren are tapped in while others are tapped out, but we need to tap into what God has called us to do so we can advance the kingdom of God on earth and push back the kingdom of darkness. Some Christians, when they experience trials and tribulations, don't pursue spiritual warfare in the spirit and strength of the Lord; they tap out and say that's enough. We have to tap in. We are in the last days, and so many of us are tapped out to the voice and power of God. We are not aware of the spiritual battle raging against our lives, families, walk with God, and calling of God. We are letting the rulers of darkness blind our eyes to the spiritual warfare that is taking place in our minds. We are letting distractions, personal motives, fear, and intimidation cause us to tap out of doing the work that God has called us to. The Bible declares that many are called, but few are chosen, because so many are deceived, blinded, and doing their own thing (paraphrased Matthew 22:14).

We are doing things in our own strength and not the calling, strength, and Spirit of God. What we are endeavoring should glorify God and not ourselves. God should be the center of everything that we do, and if He is not, we need to re-evaluate. If we are doing things in our own strength and zeal, personal motives and ambition, and not according to what God has told us to do. We are living a lifestyle that is conformed to this world and culture when the Bible tells us in Romans 12:2 (KJV): "And do not be conformed to this world, but be ye transformed by the renewing of your mind, that you may prove what is that good and acceptable and perfect will of God."

When we walk according to our own strength, that's when we tap out because we can't accomplish what God wants us to do in our own strength. We have to walk in the calling of God, in the strength and power of God. The scripture says in Zechariah 4:6 (KJV): "Not by might, nor by power, but by My Spirit, says the Lord of hosts." We gain our strength to accomplish God's will and calling when we do all things in the spirit of the Lord. When we are in the spirit, that's when we hear the voice of God clearly. That's when we are connected to God. That's when I'm walking in obedience to God. The Bible tells us to walk in the Spirit. For God is a spirit, and we must worship God in spirit and in truth. When we walk in the Spirit, we have life and peace. When we walk according to the flesh, it's death. When we do things with our own strength, that's when we get worn out and tap out of the spiritual fight. The Bible tells us to fight a good fight and that we are soldiers in the army of the Lord: "Fight the good fight of faith. Take hold of the eternal life to which you were called when you made your good confession in the presence of many witnesses" (1 Timothy 6:12, NIV). It is not time to tap out, but to tap in to fight the good fight of faith.

Now, how do we Spiritually Tap In?

By putting on the armor of God.

[10] Finally, be strong in the Lord and in his mighty power. [11] Put on the full armor of God, so that you can take your stand against the devil's schemes. [12] For our struggle is not against flesh and blood, but against the rulers, against the authorities, against the powers of this dark world and against the spiritual forces of evil in the heavenly realms. [13] Therefore put on the full armor of God, so that when the day of evil comes, you may be able to stand your ground, and after you have done everything, to stand. [14] Stand firm then, with the belt of truth buckled around your waist, with the breastplate of righteousness in place, [15] and with your feet fitted with the readiness that comes from the gospel of peace. [16] In addition to all this, take up the shield of faith, with which you can extinguish all the flaming arrows of the evil one. [17] Take the helmet of salvation and the sword of the Spirit, which is the word of God.

—Ephesians 6:10-17, NIV

Prayer

In all things, pray. Prayer builds up your spirit.

[18] And pray in the Spirit on all occasions with all kinds of prayers and requests. With this in mind, be alert and always keep on praying for all the Lord's people.

—Ephesians 6:18, NIV

Reading the Word

Study to show thyself approved unto God, a workman that needed not to be ashamed, rightly dividing the word of truth.

—2 Timothy 2:15, KJV

Walking in the Spirit

So I say, walk by the Spirit, and you will not gratify the desires of the flesh.

—Galatians 5:16

In closing, once we do all things to stand firm and tap in, then we can say, "I have fought a good fight, I have finished my course, I have kept the faith" (2 Timothy 4:7, KJV).

Day Twenty:
Called by God. It's Not Time to Give Up

[1] One day as Jesus was standing by the Lake of Gennesaret, the people were crowding around him and listening to the word of God. [2] He saw at the water's edge two boats, left there by the fishermen, who were washing their nets. [3] He got into one of the boats, the one belonging to Simon, and asked him to put out a little from shore. Then he sat down and taught the people from the boat.

[4] When he had finished speaking, he said to Simon, "Put out into deep water, and let down the nets for a catch."

[5] Simon answered, "Master, we've worked hard all night and haven't caught anything. But because you say so, I will let down the nets."

[6] When they had done so, they caught such a large number of fish that their nets began to break. [7] So they signaled their partners in the other boat to come and help them, and they came and filled both boats so full that they began to sink.

[8] When Simon Peter saw this, he fell at Jesus' knees and said, "Go away from me, Lord; I am a sinful man!" [9] For he and all his companions were astonished at the catch of fish they had taken, [10] and so were James and John, the sons of Zebedee, Simon's partners.

Then Jesus said to Simon, "Don't be afraid; from now on you will fish for people." [11] So they pulled their boats up on shore, left everything and followed him.

—Luke 5:1-11, NIV

God brought to my attention how powerful a mother's words are for her children. And God wants us to understand that this connection and relationship with a mother's words is reflective of how words can shape and change our lives. This scripture shows the power and depth of God's Word. God is saying for us to hold on because a Word from heaven is on the way to uplift, encourage, renew, and strengthen us when we least expect it.

At the very moment when you want to give up and throw in the towel, words can change the trajectory of your life. The words spoken to Peter transitioned him from an observer to a follower of God who walked intimately with God.

For God's strength is made perfect in our weakness, for when we are weak, then are we strong.

—2 Corinthians 12:9, KJV

When you're weak, that's when you have to fix your eyes on God, lean into Him, and abide contrary to the situation or what the enemy is telling you.

To go deeper into God, the Holy Spirit highlights several points from this passage of scripture that will encourage you not to give up and go deeper into God:

Verse Four: Hear God's Voice

Proximity to hear God's voice. What's hindering us from going deeper in Christ is that we are not in close proximity to Him. The first request from God to Peter was to use what he had: his boat. I can't be distracted by past failures or distractions. If I find myself in the right posture before the Lord, then I can hear Him speak to me.

The Bible says in John 10:27 (KJV): "My sheep hear my voice, and I know them, and they follow me." We hear God's voice by abiding in Him, resting in His Word, and being obedient to God, because obedience is more than sacrifice.

The words Jesus spoke to him changed the entire trajectory of his life. No longer was he an observer of Jesus, but he became a follower of God and walked intimately with Jesus.

Verse Five: Believe What God Says and Obey

To go deeper into God, I have to silence doubt and skepticism. I have to learn how to walk in faith. "For we walk by faith, not by sight" (2 Corinthians 5:7, KJV). When Jesus speaks those words to Peter to go out into the deep and let down his net for a catch, Peter responds to God's Word, saying that he has toiled all night and caught nothing. This is when the enemy wants you to look at your situation and not walk in faith and give up based on what you currently see in your current circumstance.

This is when we have to believe God and do what He says. We have to walk and act in agreement with the Word of God over our situation.

> *God is not a man, that he should lie;*
> *neither the son of man, that he should repent:*
> *hath he said, and shall he not do it?*
>
> *—Numbers 23:19, KJV*

> *And he said, The things which are impossible with men*
> *are possible with God.*
>
> *—Luke 18:27, KJV*

Even when I'm tired, I believe Your Word is true. We have to take God at His Word. Just as Peter said, "Nevertheless, at thy word, I will let down my net." We have to develop a "nevertheless" mentality. It's a belief system that God's Word will do what He says

His Word will do. "No word from God will ever fail" (Luke 1:37, KJV). We have to believe that God watches over His Word to perform it.

Verse Six: God Is a Backer of His Word

When God speaks His Word, everything in creation has to come into alignment with that Word: fish, wind, waves, your body, my mind, and so on. And we see this here in the text: Peter was fishing all day and caught nothing, but when the Lord said, "Let down your net," He spoke His Word to Simon/Peter that the fish then heard and came into alignment with.

So, when God speaks health and wholeness over a cancer-ridden body, no matter what the enemy says, it's null and void. When God speaks, it is done. There is life and death in the power of our words.

When you walk in obedience, the invisible becomes visible. Peter casting his net over and over again metaphorically represents us living an empty life going through the phases of everyday life—not connected and not living an abundant life that God has called us to. Every day, pulling up an empty net, living a life he was not called to. How many of us are finding ourselves in the same position as Peter? Casting empty nets and not realizing that the empty net represents us not walking in our calling and purpose?

Some of you have been casting your net, and it's been coming back empty. And I sense your frustration and disappointment, but this season, wait to cast your net until you get a Word from God. Because God is telling you to wait on Him because when He tells you to cast your net, it's going to come back to you full, overflowing. So don't quit, don't give up; just change your strategy and whom you are listening to. The enemy can't stop the call of God on your life. But he can do things to distract you and plant thoughts into your mind that get you off the call of God on your life. Don't give up; faith is the substance of things hoped for and the evidence of things not seen.

Verse Seven: Those Around You Are Going to Be Blessed Because of Your Obedience

Those who are obedient to the Word of God will see the blessings and miracles of the Lord. Scripture says, "The blessing of the Lord, it maketh rich, and he addeth no sorrow with it" (Proverbs 10:22, KJV). Not only is God going to bless you, but those connected to you are also going to experience this abundance—your generation and the generation after you.

Verse Eight: Peter Fell to His Knees, Saying, "Depart from Me. I'm a Sinful Man"

God performed the miracle so that Peter would believe in Him. And to build up his faith. God already knows we are shapen in iniquity and that Peter is a sinful man, but He still calls and wants Peter to serve. He still has a plan and purpose for you. What you did or have done is not going to change the calling of God in your life. If any man is in Christ, he is a new creation. Old things pass away; all things become new. God is going to do something new in his/your life and through him.

Call unto me, and I will show you great and mighty things, which thou knowest not.

—Jeremiah 33:3, KJV

Verse Ten: God Calls Peter

...Fear not; from henceforth thou shalt catch men.

—Luke 5:10, KJV

God saw Peter and called him before the foundation of the world. Like He sees you and has called you before the foundation of the world. When God spoke those words to Peter, He was telling him that this was not the only thing He was going to do in his life; greater things he shall do and see: "To take you deep in me, I'm going to reveal my glory to you and who I am before any of the other disciples have a revelation of me. You're going to do things that no other disciple does." When you look at the life of Peter, he is the disciple who walked on water. Peter was with God on the Mount of Transfiguration. Peter's shadow heals the sick. Peter's life and calling epitomize what God sees in you even when you don't see anything. David puts it this way in Psalm 139:16 (NKJV): "Your eyes saw my substance, being yet unformed. And in your book, they all were written, the days fashioned for me, when as yet there were none of them."

Those God calls, He names.

God changed his name from Simon to Peter ("Cephas," which translates to "rock" or "stone") (paraphrased John 1:42, KJV).

"And I also say to you that you are Peter, and on this rock I will build My church; and the gates of Hades shall not prevail against it" (Matthew 16:18, KJV).

Day Twenty-One:
Quiet the Storm

³⁵ That day when evening came, he said to his disciples, "Let us go over to the other side." ³⁶ Leaving the crowd behind, they took him along, just as he was, in the boat. There were also other boats with him. ³⁷ A furious squall came up, and the waves broke over the boat, so that it was nearly swamped. ³⁸ Jesus was in the stern, sleeping on a cushion. The disciples woke him and said to him, "Teacher, don't you care if we drown?"

³⁹ He got up, rebuked the wind and said to the waves, "Quiet! Be still!" Then the wind died down and it was completely calm.

⁴⁰ He said to his disciples, "Why are you so afraid? Do you still have no faith?"

⁴¹ They were terrified and asked each other, "Who is this? Even the wind and the waves obey him!"

—Mark 4:35-41, NIV

There are seasons in our lives that are very turbulent and make us feel like we are in the eye of a storm. Not everybody enters a storm at the same time. It's seasons that we go in and out of. Some of you who are reading this devotional now are in the eye of the storm, and God desires for you to go through that storm with His divine peace. Scripture declares in John 14:27 (NIV): "Peace I leave with you; my peace I give you. I do not give to you as the world gives. Do not let your hearts be troubled and do not be afraid."

God is telling us not to be afraid no matter what the situation may feel or look like. God gives us a promise in His Word in Isaiah 26:3 (NIV): "God will keep you in perfect peace those whose mind is steadfast, because they trust in [H]im." God does not want us to be tossed to and fro and shaken by the storms of life. He wants us to be steadfast and grounded in faith. To rest and trust in His sovereignty in the storms of life because He is our sure foundation, the very rock upon which we stand. God desires for us to hold fast to the profession of faith without wavering, because He is faithful that promised, especially in the storms of life. When we are facing the storms of life, we have to speak and stand on the promises of God in faith. God is the "author and finisher" of our faith, and He will perfect that which is lacking in our faith. We just have to stand and believe His Word and the precious promises he has given to us.

We see here in this particular passage of scripture that the disciples are on a journey with Jesus and have experienced a strong storm. When they departed, the seas were normal, but now, out of nowhere, they are not just in a physical storm, but a spiritual one that is threatening their lives, and the very person that could do something about it is peacefully sleeping on the boat, not physically aware of the detrimental situation they are in. The Bible says a squall comes upon them. The Oxford Dictionary defines "squall" as a violent gust of wind bringing rain. So much rain is causing the boat to sink. As they are emptying the water from the boats, buckets of rain fill the boat.

Peter sees that human effort cannot do anything to save them, and out of fear, he goes and wakes up Jesus because he knows He could do something about the situation. Sometimes, in our storms, we respond to Jesus the same as Peter, not believing that God is more than able to handle any situation we are experiencing. Just like the disciples, we let fear talk to our situation instead of faith and our belief in who God is. We speak out of fear, and God desires us to speak out of faith in the midst of the storm. God desires for us to stand on the promises of God. Meaning that we don't bow to our circumstances, but our circumstances bow to the promises of God. God's Word declares that He will preserve you in the promises of God. The Word declares, "...his faithful promises are your armor and protection" (Psalm 91:4, NLT).

When Jesus awakens, He looks at the disciples and sees that this is a situation His disciples have been empowered to handle, but lacked faith to do so. But Jesus does not address His disciples first; He addresses the storm. We can perceive that the winds are caused by the supernatural because when Jesus gets up, He rebukes the wind and speaks to the sea. To rebuke something means an expression of sharp disapproval and criticism, according to the Oxford Dictionary. The word rebuke is often used in scripture to cast out demons. Even though the enemy knows he can't take you out without God's permission, he will still try to place obstacles in your path to threaten and instill fear in you. The ship was not going to be swallowed or capsized by the waves. Yet still, the enemy wants you to think that what you are going through is life-threatening or detrimental. The Word declares in 1 Peter 5:8 (NIV): "Be alert and of sober mind. Your enemy the devil prowls around like a roaring lion looking for someone to devour." The word declares in John 10:10 KJV, "The thief cometh not, but for to steal, kill and to destroy; I am come that that they might have life, and that they might have it more abundantly".

The disciples watched God cast out demons, open blind eyes, heal the sick, and perform all sorts of miracles, yet they thought He would forsake them and let them drown. But fear will make you talk and think crazy. Fear can cause a person to doubt the power of the very God you walk with.

The enemy has the power to act in this earthly realm, but he does not have authority; all his actions have to be approved by God. So, he can send the winds to shake you, but God, our sure foundation, will rise to our defense and rebuke the winds and speak to the sea. This means that for any situation in your life that seems hopeless, God will speak a word of peace into your storm and quiet every storm in your life.

The winds we experience in our lives are to get us to take our focus off of God. To get us off track of His purpose. The storm is to delay your purpose and call and instill a paralyzing fear within you. Cast your fears aside and stand in faith that God has equipped you with everything you need to survive the storm.

In closing, God is telling you to rebuke the winds, speak to the sea, and continue in what God has called and purposed you to do. So, when you are faced with the storms of life, keep your peace and stand in faith that God will not forsake you in the storm, but has equipped you with enough faith to move through the storm in the peace of God.

Bonus:
Day Twenty-Two:
Way of Escape

¹³ No temptation has overtaken you except such as is common to man; but God is faithful, who will not allow you to be tempted beyond what you are able, but with the temptation will also make the way of escape, that you may be able to bear it.

—1 Corinthians 10:13, NKJV

God allows things to occur in our lives to strengthen us spiritually. We all know the story of Jesus, who, after being baptized, was led into the wilderness by the Holy Spirit to fast for forty days and be tempted by the devil. The devil came to tempt Jesus when Jesus was ready to walk in His purpose and calling. Once Jesus was baptized by John the Baptist, the heavens were opened, and the Spirit of God descended like a dove on Jesus and said, "This is my beloved Son in whom I am well pleased." Once the enemy got word of who Jesus was and of Him walking into His ministry, the enemy's main goal was to tempt Him to see if this was actually God. This is why, with every temptation, the devil said, "If you are the Son of God." The enemy used the information heard to question what he had heard and who Jesus was.

Secondly, the enemy tempts you when you are at your weakest moment. The enemy waited for Jesus to be weak and hungry after the forty-day fast to tempt Him. The enemy waited for Jesus to finish the fast to tempt Him in His weakest moments. The first thing we need to know is that God does not tempt men. It is the strategy of the enemy to tempt mankind. The enemy will use what interests you and your weakness to tempt you. His goal is to use temptation to lure you into his deception to destroy you. The Bible declares in John 10:10 (KJV): "The thief comes to steal, kill and destroy but God came to give you life and give it to you more abundantly." The enemy tempts mankind to destroy us. In comparison, God cannot tempt you. God is not a tempter of mankind. God will TEST you, meaning that He will test you based on your strengths to elevate you to the next level. "Fire tests the purity of silver and gold, but the Lord tests the heart" (Proverbs 17:3, NLT). God desires for us to grow when we are tested by Him. "Behold, I have refined you, but not as silver; I have tested you in the furnace of affliction" (Isaiah 48:10, KJV). Because God desires for us to live an abundant life, a "Zoë" life, which is Greek for an abundant life. God tests us to see if we can pass the test that He has placed in front of us. "I, the Lord, search the heart, I test the mind, Even to give to each man according to his ways, and according to the fruit of his doings" (Jeremiah 17:10, KJV). God tests your strengths to elevate you to the next spiritual level in Him, whereas the enemy tempts you based on your weaknesses to destroy you and separate you from God. The goal of the enemy is to use temptation to pull you away from the presence of God.

What happens to those who are not living in the Spirit is that they begin to look for and fall prey to temptation because they are not strong spiritually or walking in the Spirit. So they use their own strength and reasoning to make their way of escape and not depend on God.

We need to wait on God to provide a way of escape when we are faced with temptation from the enemy. Let me say that again: we need to wait on God. And while waiting on God, we need to stand strong in the Word and resist the devil. The scripture declares in James 4:7 (KJV): "Submit to God, resist the devil, and he will flee from you." When we do this, we will see God take every temptation or weapon that the enemy has formed against us and turn it into testimony, strengthening our praise and intimacy with Him.

Salvation

If the words in this devotional inspired you by the Holy Spirit, it is your time to dedicate and give your life to Christ so that He can dwell in you. You can't live a life in the Spirit unless you are connected to the vine, Jesus. He has to make his abode in you. You have to accept and believe that he is your Lord and Savior in order to live and walk in the Spirit. The Spirit of God is only given to those who have accepted Jesus as their Lord and Savior. Today is the day to accept the Lord, and if you would like to invite him into your heart, confess these words aloud, and you will be brought into the Family of Christ Jesus.

Dear Lord,

I confess that I am a sinner, and I believe and declare that Jesus is my Lord and believe in my heart that Jesus died and God raised Him from the dead for me and my sins. I thank You for Your love and for Jesus, and I accept You into my life.

I invite the Holy Spirit into my life to guide me in the truth of Jesus and to fill me up.

In Jesus's Name, I pray.

Amen.

www.ingramcontent.com/pod-product-compliance
Lightning Source LLC
Chambersburg PA
CBHW071756040426
42446CB00012B/2587